James Nayler

Speaking

Brian Drayton

Pendle Hill Pamphlet 413

About the Author

Brian Drayton of Weare (NH) Monthly Meeting is a plant ecologist working in science education research, and a recorded minister in New England Yearly Meeting. He has traveled extensively under a concern to encourage Gospel ministry, and has given workshops, retreats, and addresses on topics in Quaker history and belief for monthly, quarterly, and yearly meetings and elsewhere. In 1994, he published *Selections from the Writings of James Nayler*. Other writings include *Treasure in Earthen Vessels* (1997), *On Living With a Concern for Gospel Ministry* (2006), *Getting Rooted* (Pendle Hill Pamphlet #391, 2007), and *Unity, Disunity, Diversity* (2007).

> *This essay is dedicated to Hugh Barbour, Lamb's Warrior, and to Gordon Bugbee, in gratitude to both for encouragement and guidance, and for work and learning shared.*

Publications staff: Shirley Dodson
Cover drawing by Darcy Drayton
Pamphlet edited by Chel Avery and designed by Mary Helgesen Gabel
Requests for permission to quote or to translate should be addressed to:
Pendle Hill Publications, 338 Plush Mill Road, Wallingford, PA 19086-6023
Email: publications@pendlehill.org
ISBN   978-0-87574-413-1
June 2011

James Nayler

Speaking

Art thou in darkness? Mind it not, for if thou do it will fill thee more, but stand still and act not, and wait in patience till light arise out of darkness to lead thee. Art thou wounded in conscience? Feed not there, but abide in the light, which leads to the grace and truth, which teaches to deny and put off the weight, & removes the cause, and brings saving health to light.[1]

To read James Nayler is to connect with Quakerism's initial eruption of insight and obedience, in the turmoil of the 1650s. Seekers, many of whom became Friends at last, put their hopes for a renewed world in a succession of potential solutions—separated worship, new prophets, the Parliamentary cause and the Rule of the Saints. Each in turn was found deeply wanting, yet the sense that change was needed *now*, "reformation without tarrying for any," remained. Under this tension, and in the pain of repeated loss of hope, the sense of a new possibility broke through: those who were becoming Friends found theology, politics, personality, and the meanings of history melted down and recast in the "terror and power of the Light."[2] That convicting Light, and its consolation, answered the hungers and confusions of a modernizing, pluralizing world, composed of tradition and novelty, reason and superstition, civilization and savagery, sacred and profane.[3] In this mix and the sense of urgent search, their times resemble ours.

And our times call us to a full engagement on every level. While humans are unchanged in our essentials, we encounter unprecedented conditions. Never before have we lived in a world with seven billion other people; never have we lived in a world whose resources are under such intense demand. Never have so many had at their disposal such powerful tools of communication, exploitation, creation, and destruction. In such times, it is hard not to say, with George Fox, that all our hopes in all men are gone, nor can we tell what to do.[4]

I came to James Nayler seeking insight from a pioneering spirit at the roots of Quakerism, one who found the paradoxical order and peace of the Lamb in another time of chaos. Nayler sought fiercely and with humility, thought deeply, and spoke prophetically and incisively. He helped me grapple with some of the questions I had about life as a Quaker: When we say we are spirit-led, what spirit is leading us? How do we realize in our times the demands and promises of Christ's covenant? How is our inward struggle toward faithfulness and unity connected to the outward work of reconciliation? My hope with this essay is to introduce modern Friends to Nayler's writings, his voice and ideas, so that they may be encouraged or intrigued to read more of his writings themselves and engage in dialogue with this powerful, resourceful, and disturbing Quaker founder.

*Q*uakerism as preached in the first generations cannot be well captured in an enumeration of "issues" that Friends addressed, such as equality, religious toleration, or peace. It was a prophetic elaboration of the realization that Christ's spirit is present, active, and reliably knowable by all who seek it. By its nature it contradicts many conventional values, offering a kind of freedom and power that can actually overcome evil, both inward and outward. This offer can be accepted by a unique spiritual method, epitomized for me by the phrases *mind the Light* and *living in the Cross*. The Quaker vision makes claims about human nature, about the nature of the Divine, and about divine-human relationships. These claims amount to a narrative about the soul's life which had compelling energy in the day of its first preaching and gave Quakerism a scope for which it seems we modern Friends long.

But Nayler's writings and his life also give us valuable teaching about how hard it is to live under the direct, perceptible guidance of the Spirit—how hard and how glorious—and demonstrate that the difficulty and the glory are two sides of the same coin. Relying on the present life of Christ, inwardly active and known, we can be free from fear, liberated to complete faithfulness in the life of God, enabled to taste the flowing, inexhaustible life of the Light, the Word, the Life, and Wisdom of God, given inerrant insight into the ways of sin and of salvation, and rewarded and surprised by joy unknown by the uncomprehending world, as well as baptized into sorrow and mourning for the Seed's oppression wherever found.

Modern Friends are not so likely to claim these sky-scraping exaltations and attainments. Long experience has made us familiar with the pitfalls and mazes that await those who claim the Spirit's guidance too easily.[5] How shall I know the Spirit's voice, as different from my own? Which Spirit is it that I should be hearing, and how may I recognize it? How if there are conflicting views? What if I, or my friend, or my meeting, forget how to hear the Guide? Or what if we just lose the habit of listening, let our Friendship wither by neglect or the cares of life—how then can we regain our savor? Why is it so hard to live up to the Light I think I have been given, and how shall I deal with failure of my good intentions?

Nayler engages us with the true complexity of life with the Spirit. He reminds us that the Light brings both disturbance and reassurance, both conviction and consolation. Both the trouble and the healing are essential elements of its life and action. It is tempting, comfortable, and very modern to mute or regulate our availability to both aspects of life with the Spirit of Christ. How impoverished my soul has been, in exchange for that comfort!

Nayler's Life

James Nayler was born in Yorkshire in 1618 (he was thus six years older than George Fox).[6] His family were husbandmen (one account gives his father's occupation as "hog gelder," but the evidence suggests a solid farming establishment), in the area around Wakefield (about 35 miles southwest of York), and James farmed as well. He married his wife Anne about 1639 and they had three daughters.

In his twenties he joined Cromwell's New Model Army, a breeding ground for radical thinking and radical religion. Nayler held the responsible post of quartermaster. A careful study by David Neelon has shown that Nayler was both competent as a leader and steward and ardent in his commitment to the more radical view of the Parliamentary cause.[7] Nayler was one of those whose gifts as a lay preacher were called out during their service in Cromwell's army, and no doubt the lively discussions about religion and politics honed his skills in debate as well.

He left the army, probably because of illness, and went back to his farm. His religious search continued, and he joined himself to an independent congregation in the area. During this time, as he clarified his thought and examined his inward experience, he had an intimation that he might be called out to search and to testify to the work of Christ and the decisive nature of the nation's spiritual crisis. In 1652 he met with George Fox, and this encounter must have been an encouragement to his sense of urgent calling, though James's account does not give George so decisive a role. It seems that James had already come to a place of substantial harmony with Fox's position and was ready to find and join with a movement of others called in the same direction. The disparity between the two men's accounts of the event of Nayler's call is perhaps significant in the light of the intense, almost sibling-like, relationship that developed between them.

James quickly became recognized as a leader of the movement and had very wide service in the North of England, often collaborating with George Fox. He became a prolific and effective pamphleteer, ably disputing the opponents of Quakerism and often taking part in public debates. He was seen by some as the most important leader among Friends, and his personal appeal was quite powerful.

In the mid-1650s Friends began their "campaign" on London and the other southerly cities, and James was among several prominent Friends who came to bring their message to the capital. During much of 1655-56, James was a focal point for the London work, preaching, counseling, and writing at a ferocious pace, often with little help and little break. Letters from the time give intimations of the strain that was building in James, along with rejoicing about the way the work was prospering in the great metropolis. Both moods were of concern to his colleagues, as is seen in some of the letters among the Publishers of Truth preserved from this time. The sense of pressure and perhaps exhaustion during this time of great labor was exacerbated in James's case by the fact that he was ascetic in many of his practices and (like others of the time) used fasts as both penance and spiritual nourishment.

Extended fasting, overwork, and a kind of exaltation in the success of the London mission can perhaps explain in some measure James's susceptibility to the adulation given him by a small group of enthusiasts, predominantly women. It was common at the time for grateful souls to address their spiritual heroes in rather extravagant language, but James was not in a condition to see that the praise and ecstasy aimed at him as a presentment of the living Christ were having spiritually deluding effects on his followers and even himself.

Events continued in a downward spiral during 1656. James was prevailed upon to come to a gathering of leading Friends in Bristol. During this meeting, though Friends were distressed by his state, they still held him in great confidence and clearly were praying and hoping for him to recover his equilibrium. At their urging, he set out from Bristol to visit Fox, who was lying in jail in Launceston. Nayler was apprehended on the way and thrown into prison at Exeter. During this period, he undertook an extended and severe fast. During his incarceration, and after his release, his followers carried on a campaign of dissent and disruption within the Quaker movement. Several sorry interchanges, by letter and in person, between Nayler and the hard-pressed Fox, increased the sense of distance that had grown between James and his closest friends in the movement. Nayler would not reprove his followers, and moreover grew increasingly resentful of the reproofs he received from other leaders in the movement. The distress and concern felt among Friends was very great; partisan feelings intensified and fear also grew for the young movement itself, as Nayler's prominence as preacher and apologist made his possible fall a very grave matter indeed.

In the fall of 1656, James was led in a sorry reenactment of Jesus's entry into Jerusalem through the gates of Bristol, with his little band of followers calling "Holy, Holy, Holy, Lord God of Hosts." He was arrested, and in an irregular process eventually tried and convicted as a blasphemer by Parliament itself. Studies by Bittle and Damrosch make clear the forces at work to produce such a bizarre turn of events. [8] James was publicly humiliated, severely tortured, and incarcerated for the rest of the decade.

The Quaker movement was scandalized in every sense of the word. Critics could point to Nayler as proof that Friends and Ranters were kindred extravagant spirits at bottom and that they were a danger to the souls and the peace of the kingdom. Leaders among Friends were brought to see how their spirituality could be deceived and derailed by too great a trust that inward movements were all Christ's doing, and much of the system of corporate discernment and Quaker caution dates from Friends' attempts to absorb the lessons of "Nayler's fall." We are still living with the aftereffects.

George Fox saw in this episode the seeds of ruin for all that he had labored to build; it was very long before he was brought to a formal reconciliation with James. He had statesmanlike reasons for trying to restrain James and later to distance himself from the Nayler group; Fox also was personally affronted by James's unwillingness to acknowledge Fox's preeminence. It can be plausibly argued that he never really forgave James, and the incident and its implications affected his response to later controversies and extravagancies. God only knows what his inward state was, in the end. He claimed on his deathbed that he was fully clear, and one can only hope that this included the wounds from his relationship with Nayler, the betraying brother. Much has been said about their relationship and its consequences, and much still remains unknown.

James was released from prison in 1659. He had, some years before, been reconciled to many Friends, had published apologies and recantations for his behavior and its effects on Friends and their enemies, and had regained his sense of balance and commitment to the Truth he had published so effectively before. He took up his ministry again. Friends said his testimony was as powerful as ever, and perhaps it had especial effect and depth because of his great trials. He was on his way to visit his family in Yorkshire in 1660. (He had seen his wife sporadically from time to time in the past decade, and she came at crucial times to offer comfort or support, but she had remained to work on the farm, with hired help.) On his way home, he was waylaid on the highway, beaten, and robbed; he died soon afterwards. He had been a Friend for about eight years.

Some Key Ideas in Nayler's Writings

Nayler's writings are extensive. They take several forms, including prophetic and pastoral messages, theological tracts, letters, and answers and challenges to opponents. His theology was formulated under prophetic concern, in declaration or debate, rooted not in scholarship but in his experience of and reflections on Christ's work and nature as well as human nature and behavior.[9] Though he is often notably logical, systematic, and clear in his thinking, he did not sit down to compose formal theological treatises in the way that Barclay did.[10] Yet certain key ideas are to be found throughout his writings, providing an underlying coherence of thought and language which reflects his clarity and focus to powerful effect. Furthermore, his consistent concern for souls, his awareness of the subtleties of inward experience, result in passages of great sweetness and insight, reminiscent of some of Isaac Penington's writings on the inner life.

Christ not a "meaning," but alive and fresh-born among us. Nayler, like the other early Friends, saw how easily people substitute ideas about Christ for the living Word, the inward Birth. Seeking always to know and heed the true Christ's voice is the foundation of all. To allow oneself to continue in deceit is to yield to a false, self-shaped God.

> This [human-centered] spirit serves himself with a meaning instead of serving Christ with real actual obedience. And so his birth is a meaning instead of the life of Christ.[11]

To Nayler, this inward appearing and work of the Christ-life is concrete, visceral, and the most precious fact of human existence. The early Friends meditated on it and sought out its implications in a hundred different ways. It was the beginning of a joyous walk to freedom from sin and death, to feel the Presence with you always. The steady consciousness of this transcendent, transpersonal life also brought warning—do not claim it for yourself, do not try to manage it, do not forget the simple truth of this Life. At first it brought judgment and fear: How can I possibly give it welcome, being what I am? How can the pure and holy take up residence in such a habitation? It brought pain, as well: How often I have betrayed it, wandered away from its embrace and light! How much in my life disables me from being in its friendship and joy!

But the spirit of Christ, while it brings judgment by its nature (see John, chapters 4 and 5, for example), is also a spirit of invitation, forgiveness, and healing. It gives power to become God's children (John 1:12–13) and comes simply requesting hospitality: "Behold, I stand at the door and knock" (Rev. 3:20). Beyond all thinking, contending, preaching, doing, and withholding, there is first the simple acceptance of invitation and of enduring companionship, even sometimes when hope makes no sense:

> Dear Hearts, you make your own troubles, by being unwilling and disobedient to that which would lead you. I see there is no way but to go hand in hand with him in all things, running after him without fear or considering, leaving the whole work only to him. If he seem to smile, follow him in fear and love; and if he seem to frown, follow him, and fall into his will, and you shall see he is yours still.[12]

Two seeds, two births. In each of us, there is a seed that originates from God, which can form the basis of the birth and burgeoning of Christ within.[13] This little seed has much about it which is inviting, but it needs to be cherished and cultivated, because its life often is in opposition to human preferences or tendencies of emotion, body, or culture. Yet there is also another seed, which is opposed to that divine seed, which also ramifies as a source of motivation, as a mode of thinking, as the ground of judgment. It is likely to grow unless opposed, because it is in harmony with, is fed by, the impulses of our bodies, the institutionalized wrongs in our cultures, the delusive security of mental constructs.

Where the life rooted in one seed predominates, the other life is repressed and in time will be eliminated. While we are yet uncommitted and subject to the influence of both, we can feel the two kinds of life at work within and see their fruits in our behavior—now sometimes righteous, now sometimes unrighteous.

At first, both impulses are indeed like seeds, tiny and potential, their first stages of growth subtle and hard to detect. We are likely to discount their importance and overlook the power that they can come to have. So little a source of evil cannot be taken seriously, and so it can gain strength while we indulge it; so little a source of good, the seed of God, is not taken seriously, because it seems weak, quiet, and vulnerable, and to cultivate it we must bend low, listen sharply, wait faithfully, and cherish every fruit it bears. Often, as with other Quaker authors, "seed" for Nayler is not (solely) an agricultural image, but an image of animal (and spiritual) procreation, and so he talks of two births, a birth from above (as if by the seed of God), and the birth from below (as if from the fallen nature).

The idea, in any case, is that from a small beginning, life of a particular quality can grow and achieve power in one's mind and heart and bear fruit in behavior that is consonant with its origins, but it may not be discernible at the very first, unless one looks with clear spiritual vision. As with the fruit, stem, leaves, and roots of a plant, all are of a piece, all parts have a common stream of life, which supports continued growth and hardiness in the way already taken.[14]

> Now he that believes salvation, and that cleaves to, and lives in some sin, and pleads for it, and believes he must do so, his faith stands in an unclean thing, and an unclean thing will live by that faith, and be justified by that creature; and in his justifying anything that is unclean, the

wild plant has its liberty to grow until it overspread the Plant of God, and cover the man, wholly stop the ear, and blind the eye, and hardens the heart against every motion to good, or check for evil; and lets not this man look for good fruit, but after his faith who so believes.

Also, on the contrary, he that feels a strife in himself between the clean and the unclean, and sees the one reprove for sin, and the other plead for sin, and believes in that which is pure, clean and just, which condemns the unjust and unclean, that faith stands in that which is pure, and the mystery of it is held in a pure conscience; and that pure faith being followed, will purify the heart, and cleanses the hands from unjust actions; and by that faith the Just lives, and grows and springs, and brings forth, and the pure Plant spreads and covers the earth with the knowledge of God, His holiness and purity, and all grace in the heart, which becomes as a working leaven, till it has wrought out the unclean nature, and conformed the whole man to himself; and this is a work of the holy faith, which none can receive, but who believes in holiness; for none can bring clean fruit out of an unclean faith.[15]

Thus, Nayler argues that, given our nature, we are deeply accessible to the power of sin; there is no sense in which we are "basically good," because we are just as basically bad. God seeks to overcome the evil in the human heart but requires our cooperation, our response to the invitation offered by the divine Seed. Note, too, how Nayler depicts the growing Christ-life at work. Here, the climate created by the faithful first decision to accept the divine birth gives inward welcome to the Just One. This puts it differently from the usual teaching, as expressed, for example, by Habakkuk, who teaches that "the just [person] shall live by faithfulness" (Hab. 2:4). Nayler says rather that it is the Just One who is enabled to indwell the faithful when they stand "in that which is pure."[16]

Once we have set out on this path, we are called to an all-or-nothing commitment. Even if we sometimes fall back, our allegiance must be clear in our own mind, and we must avail ourselves of the discipline and empowerment which God offers to those who have made this choice. "Take heed of halting between God and the world: what agreement can there be, or what peace, while you are married to the world?"[17]

The dualism that marks early Quaker theology, culture, and anthropology (understanding of human nature) is a hard thing for a modern person to relate to. We have felt it important to assert that the flesh and the soul are not separated, nor antagonistic, but are united and form a continuum. The more we learn about the exquisite interactions between mind and body, the more this duality seems contrary to wisdom. As a biologist, I am moved by the beauty of the emerging picture of the mind/body relation. I have not found it to challenge my faith at all, only to increase the sense of mystery and wonder. Early Friends, and Nayler prominent among them, spoke insistently (and shockingly in their time) about the experience of incarnation—Christ's, yes, in the life of Jesus, but also the presence and work of his Spirit in our own bodies as well, from which flow many of our challenges and blessings in the life of the spirit.

> Christ Jesus, the Immanuel, him alone I confess . . . for whose sake I have denied whatever was dear to me in this world, that I might win him and be found in him, and not in my self, whose life and virtue I find daily manifest in my mortal body . . . whom alone I seek to serve in spirit, soul, and body, night and day.[18]

However, I also find the doctrine, the world view, of the two seeds, or the two births, to be very powerful, because it is a clear reflection of the demand of the Gospels to be born again, this time of the Spirit, as well as a reminder of the real possibility that I can grow away from God. I take this to be a call to allow myself to be gradually reclaimed and renewed by a steady interchange of divine initiative and human response. Furthermore, I need to reckon with the very human tendency to delude myself about my faithfulness and strength. We often make a good start but do not persist in turning into practical fact the good intentions we form. Our initial delighted acceptance of Gospel clarity (as in the parable of the sower) takes little root and withers under the test.

> All mind your guide within you, even the pure light of God, which bears witness against all our ungodly ways, ungodly words, thoughts, works, and worships, which are after the world, and leads you without from the Lord your guide.[19]

Finally, the sometimes alien language, which speaks of things like "the spirit of the world" or the "first birth from below," conveys an important insight which we can recognize in more modern garb. We are embedded deeply in our culture. Indeed, we could hardly discover our individual selves without the tools and structures that our culture provides us, and to a large extent our thoughts, feelings, and insights take place within this framework. So all-encompassing, and so invisible is it, like the air we breathe, that its guidance and boundaries—its power over us—are hardly discernible, yet all the more effective for that. Consequently, an important part of the spiritual journey involves coming to see where and how we are called to separate ourselves from this all-encompassing incubator. This seeing, this work of moving into a life shaped by an allegiance to the Light, by an alliance to the life of Christ felt working in us, is a re-birth indeed.

True knowledge, true worship. Thus we are challenged to examine *what* we know, and *how:* the nature and source of our knowledge (1Cor. 2; James 3:14–18). Nayler suggests that the life from which we learn shapes what lessons we can receive. If we are rooted in the first birth, allied with the human delight in its own creations and values, all we can reckon with and recognize are matters, values, and methods that comport with such a life. It is allied with what is temporary, fallible, and delusive. Therefore, it necessarily must be defensive, prideful, and hardened against instruction.

> The first man is of the earth earthly; minds earthly things, lives in the earth, delights in the earth; . . . his treasure is in the earth, and his heart is with it: for it is his portion, and his thoughts, words and wisdom are all employed about it . . . [he] is never satisfied, but is a servant to it; it is his life, his joy; and if it be taken from him, his comfort is gone: it is his god, and he worships it, and would have all to worship him, because of the abundance of it that he has got together; for he knows no other God, nor greater happiness than what he sees with his carnal eyes.[20]

Because of this focus, such a person cannot engage with the living God. The form of worship most comfortable to such a person is a human construction, designed to please one's self-concept. It should not disturb one's comfort, nor awaken one to a threatening, more risky engagement with the dynamics of struggle, compassion, and witness—the Lamb's War, to which we return below.[21] Nayler's description of the condition of the person who worships by custom or convention is challenging to a modern Friend. Reading it, I am led to reflect on how often I sit in meeting with no profit but repose, going from it basically unaltered, and no further along in faithfulness than before:

> The first man worships a God at a distance, but knows Him not, nor where He is, but by relation from others, either by word or writing. And as he receives his knowledge of Him from men, so his worship towards Him is taught by the precepts of men . . . and here he has fellowship with men, or with those he calls brethren . . . but as for any command from God binding to these, or any communion with God, or answer of acceptance from Him, upon every performance, he looks for no such thing now in these days. . . . And thus in vain does he worship, receiving for doctrines the commandments of men.[22]

By contrast, the person in whom the second birth has enabled the life of Christ to arise toward ascendancy is enabled to grow out of the anxieties and narrowness of the first birth. True worship results in change toward a life more and more freed from bondage:

> Before any can rightly worship God, they must wait to know His Spirit, that leads to know Him and His worship, and the matter, and manner; for all who do the same thing only as to the outward performance, do not worship God, because they worship not in the Spirit and power of God Himself . . . the way to be well-pleasing to the Father, is to wait in the light, till you feel something of the Spirit of life, which is in Christ Jesus, moving in you, and then to that join, in its power to worship.[23]

The Progress of the Soul

For Nayler, the first inward appearing of the divine life, as in the gospel story of Jesus's birth, is small and humble. Staying faithful just to the small gifts of understanding and ability opens the door to sharper sight about how to act (or withhold action) in order to stay rooted in that life. This clearer judgment in turn shows the path to a faithfulness of greater scope. In this way, the power of Christ can come to have the victory, despite the human predilection for the concrete, immediate, and earthly:

> Standing faithful in the least measure, and waiting therein, the light of Christ under the cross, and not looking out, he is kept in peace, . . . And as the light grows, there is a discerning of things that differ, to choose the good, and refuse the evil; and as the Son arises, the judgment is brought forth: for all judgment is committed to the Son.[24]

> Thou that loves holiness, it is near thee, power over sin and Satan is near thee, salvation is at hand; go not forth to seek that abroad which thou hast lost in thy own house: he is thy salvation that condemns sin in thy bosom; he that reproves the wicked is with thee; he that is pure is thy peace; he that never consented to sin but stands a witness against it, if thou have such a spirit in thee thou hast the Spirit of Christ the savior.[25]

As one moves under the guidance of Christ's spirit, gaining clarification of judgment and transformation of behavior, opposition will arise. Some of it will arise from one's own nature or cultural formation, some from others, including friends and family. Outward opposition may include deadly persecution (from individuals or the state), as Friends were experiencing at the time Nayler wrote. Even short of that, however, one must expect to endure tension, ridicule, and rejection—and count it as evidence that one is on the right path: remember Jesus's saying, "I have come not to bring peace, but a sword" (Matt. 10:34). Thus, one's increasing openness, tenderness, and love are tested and confronted by ever fiercer challenges.

Nayler reminds us that we will recognize—both by outward and inward evidence—that the Spirit by which we are guided is the Spirit of Christ. The outward evidence arises in response to the work and presence of Christ, the prophet, the judge, the opposer of the systems of the world.

> See if your Christ be the same that was from everlasting to everlasting, or is he changed according to the times: in life, in death, in peace and wars, in reigning, in suffering, in casting out and receiving in. And if you find the true Christ then prove your faithfulness to him in all things. Doth he whom you obey as your leader lead you out to war against the world and all the pride and glory, fashions and customs, love and pleasures, and whatever is not of God therein; and to give up your lives unto death rather than knowingly to yield your obedience thereto? . . . Doth he beget in your hearts a new nature contrary to the world's nature in all things, motions, and delights like himself, whereby he works out the old nature that inclines to the world and can be at peace therein?[26]

But there is also inward evidence, the sense of Christ as healer, creator, Logos, whose power is wholly different from the power exercised by humans in ordinary life—even from that power we exercise over ourselves when we rely on our own strength to overcome what we reject.

The inward Presence is felt as blazing and revealing Light, but also as sweet, growing Life: "It is the like of gentleness, meekness, patience, and all other virtues which are of a springing and spreading nature, where they are not quenched, but suffered to come forth to His praise in His will and time, who is the Begetter thereof, and to the comfort of His own Seed, and cross to the world."[27]

This spirit as brought forth from the holy Seed is recognized by its innocence, its reliance on the invincible power of Love, which "beareth all things, believeth all things, hopeth all things, endureth all things" (1 Cor: 13:7):

> Its hope is to outlive all wrath and contention, and to weary out all exaltation and cruelty, or whatever is of a nature contrary to itself. It sees to the end of all temptations: as it bears no evil in itself, so it conceives none in thoughts to any other. If it be betrayed it bears it, for its ground and spring is the mercies and forgiveness of God. Its crown is meekness, its life is everlasting love unfeigned, and takes its kingdom with entreaty, and not with contention, and keeps it by lowliness of mind.[28]

Nayler emphasizes that the Lamb's War cannot be fought using the tools and weapons of the world. This is a hard lesson to hear and understand. Our civilization is rich in devices—physical, mental, and cultural—for getting things done in ways that damage, frighten, dominate, and arouse desire. Once we are broken open and the Seed's life is released, we will be led gently and with certainty into other ways and means.

> His kingdom in this world, in which he chiefly delights to walk and make himself known, is in the hearts of such as have believed in him, and owned his call out of the world, whose hearts he hath purified, and whose bodies

he hath washed in obedience and made them fit for the
Father to be worshipped in. And such he rejoices and
takes delight; and his kingdom in such is righteousness
and peace, in love, in power and purity. He leads them
by the gentle movings of his Spirit out of all their own
ways and wills . . . and guides them into the will of the
father, by which they become more clean and holy.[29]

While the opening can feel abrupt and traumatic, the learning is gradual, and Nayler sees God acting as a wise pedagogue,
working carefully with each of us according to our capacity:

Nor do I say, that all my sins, which formerly I had com-
mitted . . . were wholly taken away [all at once], as my
sins of ignorance were; for this I found, that God in this
was just and merciful: merciful, in that He did not lay
them all at once before me, lest they should have pressed
me down, that I could not have followed the light, nor
gotten any strength; but must needs have perished under
them.[30]

The way we participate in Christ's offer of atonement is in
this cleansing process, and the first part is the convincement of
its necessity and possibility. The second part is seeing how to
move toward the Light and rely upon its guidance. The third
and necessary part is faithfulness to what is given—and not
running beyond the Guide by anticipating more than what is
given. Both aspects of this faithfulness are essential if we are
to gain the strength in the Light that will enable us to press
forward against opposition and to bear the suffering that is the
assured consequence of living Christ's life in our own path:

Take heed of that nature that would know more than
God is willing to reveal: for you shall find that unwill-
ing to obey what it knows: and take heed of that which

desires to appear before men to be commended, for that seldom deserves praise of God.[31]

The main challenge is to stay with what we can both know (intellectually) and embody in our actions and impulses:

> Wherefore, let your food be in the life of what you know, and in the power of obedience rejoice, and not in what you know, but cannot live, for the life is the bread for your souls. . . . So let your labor and diligence be in that which presses into the heavenly Being. . . . That faith works obedience, quickness and willingness, it works out the old, and works into the new.[32]

If we stay in this teachable place, we will find a growth of understanding and of power. We will be sharper-eyed to see the often subtle, low, simple workings of the Light, God the gardener pruning and training, as well as the subtle, distracting invitations or impulses to move out of the Light and to manufacture a life that is only a counterfeit of the Kingdom. The work of the Spirit is work indeed, and as our lives are united with the Christ-life at work in us, we come to share the labor and are called to diligence while we are in the Day:

> As you mind only to feed on the Plant of life, you will come to know the work of the Father in His vineyard, and who the faithful laborer is, and what must be his work; and the slothful servant, and what his work brings forth; and the cause why the field of the sluggard is overgrown with evil fruits, and why his vineyard brings not fruit to perfection.
>
> For you will find many plants besides the tree of life, all which seek to be fed and strengthened in the mind and affections, and many grown trees tall and strong, who have got fast rooting, spread and bring forth abundantly

after their several kinds; and all these present themselves to the eye of the mind, to be fed from thence. . . .

So the work of him that is faithful is to number these to the ax, and to the fire, and not to suffer these any place in the mind, how strongly soever they tempt, and try every way to spread root to keep life; that so through the death of these, the vine may grow alone in the clean affections, and holy mind, and honest chaste heart, which is the good ground, and where the pure Plant will bring forth of itself in all, where it is not cumbered with that which is contrary to it; which contrary fruits all that mind the light may see.[33]

The Lamb's War—
Inward and Outward

*N*ayler's exposition of the Lamb's War brings to a focus all the major themes of his teaching and experience. By now the reader will have seen that in Nayler's mind the Lamb's War is a way to describe the drama of salvation. What remains to point out is that because of his understanding of God in the world, and in us, he sees that the inward struggle against "the man of sin" leads us to engage outwardly with the powers of culture, custom, and the over-reliance on human reason and competence. Thus, the Lamb that suffers conquers not only the inward kingdom, but moves ultimately to transform the outward fruits of the human heart.

The life engaged in the Lamb's War is tendered and opened to injustice and violence, outwardly as well as inwardly. The human soul, my soul, can be seen as a nexus, a confluence or focus of forces tending both to one's good and ill. Some of the evils can be seen as external—sources of fear, oppression, or distraction. Others are apparently inward—anger, self-indulgence, and so on. Yet we are so constructed that we and our environment interpenetrate. Inward and outward forces activate or counteract each other. Because it is this kind of meeting place, the human soul is an appropriate battlefield upon which to begin the war against "outward" evils in the world. More than this, if the battle remains unfought in any soul, then in our unredeemed regions, seeds of sin and death lie as in an incubator, from which they can spread abroad anew. The Lamb's War against the Man of Sin, in which we use the weapons of Jesus, acting at first upon our little, inward stage, is also a social and, indeed, revolutionary act.

Learning the path from Him, we can come to rely on His power to effect our liberation, and as the darkness is vanquished in us, we are drawn outward as well, to declare against the darkness in institutions and powers, and people:

> The end of his war is, to judge [the] deceiver openly before all the creation showing that his ways, fashions, and customs are not what God ordered for man to live in, in the beginning; to bind him and to redeem . . . out of his captivity all who will believe in the Lamb and are weary of this service and bondage to his enemy, and who will but come forth and give their names and hearts to join with him and bear his image and testimony openly before all men; . . . and all that follow him to redeem them to God.[34]

There is "no time but this present," and we must take our spiritual progress as seriously as if it were a war, the war of the Lamb against the Man of Sin. To do it, we cannot wield spiritual weapons without being in the Spirit—we cannot love another as ourselves—when our life is rooted in the first seed. "The light saith, Love thy neighbor as thyself: This the firstborn cannot do."[35] We must come down with him, to littleness and weakness as to the world, and amid the metaphors of struggle and war, we are challenged to show how utterly different the Light's way is than the way our history, our culture, our common sense command.

I have begun to understand how to join in this work by reflecting on three important motions or responses to the Light, by which we participate in the Lamb's work.

- *Waiting:* we wait not only for the first nudges of the Light, but at every step. In waiting we find both the first hints of the direction in which we should next go, but also the power to move, and bread for the journey, as required. In waiting we are given insight, too, as we cannot always recognize the needed gift right away, looking for it in a form we expect, when it may be coming as something quite fresh and unaccustomed.

- *Prompt obedience:* our way will not open completely all at once; we will be trained and led in ways we had not known before, but only if we act on what we are given, in the strength we are given, and if we keep up with the Guide. Practice makes perfect, and the gift not accepted can be withdrawn, or we may misplace it and lose its blessing.

- *Suffering:* this is a loaded term, but becomes less so if we reflect concretely on the sufferings that we have encountered when we have acted on conscience, or even started to learn a new skill. So often, the anguish or anxieties we feel are not so much physical as emotional or psychological, as we dare to change. Very often "suffering" means willingness to appear the fool and to deal in love with the conflicts that arise. But holy foolishness is of the essence of the Christian calling.

> Look at the process by which you were chosen, brothers. Not many wise according to the flesh, not many powerful, not many born to good families; but God selected the fools of the earth that they might put the wise to shame, and God chose the no-accounts that they might put those that count on trial, so that the merely earthly could not be boasting in God's presence (1 Cor. 1:26–29).[36]

The inward voice of Christ comes with both sweetness and power and with the promise that we can be transformed to such an extent that we can come (as Woolman said) to turn ourselves and all our possessions into the channel of universal love. In that love are found courage, the ability to discern and act upon the truth, and in some fashion hard to articulate, the capacity to manifest hope.

> Dear friends, be faithful in what you know, take heed of making a profession of what you are not . . . take heed of searching into the hidden things of God by your own wisdom, which is carnal, for that hath God shut out of the kingdom . . . therefore turn your minds within, and wait for a wisdom from above, which begins with the fear of the Lord, which is pure, peaceable, gentle, and easy to be entreated. And if you keep your eye to this, you shall see, as this grows, which is pure, there will be a death to that which is sensual and carnal; and as you grow in this pure, you will grow in the knowledge of Christ within you.[37]

Nayler's Account of His Calling and His Knowledge of Christ

from *Saul's Errand to Damascus*

This exchange gives a sense of Nayler in debate—from the transcript of a trial for blasphemy. There are several important points here. First is his account of his calling to publish truth—one of the few passages of autobiography we have from him. Nayler's decision to set off into service is an interesting case of the kind of inward impulse that can set an embodied spirit and mind in action. It can be taken as a true inspiration from the Holy, sometimes mistakenly so.

The second point is the sense Nayler gives of Christ alive and at work, having come a second time in spirit, present fully wherever he is found. Furthermore, the work Christ is doing now is the same work Jesus was about in the days of his earthly ministry—and the present, spiritual work is a necessary and integral part of the work begun by Jesus's life, teaching, death, and resurrection.

Col. Brigs: Where wast thou born?

James: At Ardislaw two miles from Wakefield.

Col. Brigs: How long livedst thou there?

James: Until I was married; then I went into Wakefield Parish.

Col. Brigs: What profession wast thou of?

James: A husbandman.

Col Brigs: Wast thou a soldier?

James: Yea; I was a soldier betwixt eight and nine years.

Col Brigs: Wast thou not at Burford among the Levellers?

James: I was never there.

Col. Brigs: I charge thee by the Lord, that thou tell me whether thou wast or no.

James: I was then in the north, and was never taxed for any mutiny, or any other thing, while I served the Parliament.

Col. Brigs: What was the cause of thy coming into these parts?

James: If I may have liberty, I shall declare it. I was at the plow, meditating on the things of God, and suddenly I heard a voice saying unto me, "Get thee out from thy kindred and from thy father's house"—and I had a promise given in with it. Whereupon, I did exceedingly rejoice, that I had heard the voice of that God which I had professed from a child but had never known him.

Col. Brigs: Didst thou hear that voice?

James: Yea, I did hear it; and when I came at home I gave up my estate, cast out my money; but not being obedient going forth, the wrath of God was upon me, so that I was made a wonder to all; and none thought I would have lived; but (after I was made willing) I began to make some preparation, as apparel and other necessaries, not knowing whither I should go. But shortly afterward going agateward with a friend from my own house, having on an old suit, without any money, having neither taken leave of wife or children, not thinking then of any journey, I was commanded to go into the west, not knowing whither I should go nor what I was to do there; but when I had been there a little while I had given me what I was to declare; and ever since I have remained, not knowing today what I was to do tomorrow.

Col. Brigs: What was the promise thou hadst given?

James: That God would be with me: which promise I find made good every day.

Col. Brigs: I never heard such a call as this is, in our time.

James: I believe thee.

Just. Pear: Is Christ in thee?

James: I witness him in me: and if I should deny him before men, he would deny me before my Father which is in heaven.

Just. Pear: Spiritual, you mean.

James: Yea, spiritual.

Just. Pear: By faith, or how?

James: By faith. . . .

Quest: *Was Christ man, or no?*

James: Yea, he was, and "took upon him the seed of Abraham," and was real flesh and bone; but is a mystery not known to the carnal man; for he is begotten of the "immortal seed," and those that know him, know him to be spiritual; for it was "the Word" that "became flesh, and dwelt amongst us"; and if he had not been spiritual, he had not wrought my redemption.

Just. Pear: Is Christ in thee as man?

James: Christ filleth all places, and is not divided: separate God and man, and he is no more Christ. . . .

Col. Brigs: Didst not thou write a paper wherein was mentioned, that if thou thinkest to be saved by that Christ which died at Jerusalem, thou art deceived?

James: If I cannot witness Christ nearer than Jerusalem, I shall have no benefit by him; but I own no other Christ but that who "witnessed a good confession before Pontius Pilate"; which Christ I witness suffering in me now.

ENDNOTES

1   James Nayler, "Glory to God Almighty" in *The Works of James Nayler,*
    Licia Kuenning, ed. (Glenside, PA: 2003) iv, p. 235. The Quaker
    Heritage Press, Glenside, PA, has published an edition of Nayler's
    works in four volumes, edited by Licia Kuenning. This remarkable
    work includes material not published, as well as pieces not pub-
    lished since Nayler's lifetime.

2   Hugh Barbour, *The Quakers in Puritan England* (Richmond, IN:
    Friends United Press, 1985), ch. 4.

3   Douglas Gwyn, *Seekers Found: Atonement in Early Quaker Experience*
    (Wallingford, PA: Pendle Hill Publications, 2000).

4   See George Fox, *The Journal of George Fox,* John Nickalls, ed.
    (Philadelphia: Philadelphia Yearly Meeting, 1985), p. 11.

5   For a good, concise discussion of the problem of discernment, see
    Hugh Barbour, *Limits to the Leadings of the Light* (Boston: Beacon Hill
    Friends House, 2006).

6   Revised and adapted from Brian Drayton, *Selections from the Writings
    of James Nayler,* 2nd ed. (Worcester, MA: Mosher Book and Tract
    Fund of New England Yearly Meeting, 1994).

7   See David Neelon, *James Nayler: Revolutionary to Prophet* (Becket, MA:
    Leadings Press, 2009).

8   See William Bittle, *James Nayler, the Quaker Indicted by Parliament* (York,
    England: William Sessions Ltd., 1991) and Leo Damrosch, *The Sorrows
    of the Quaker Jesus: James Nayler and the Puritan Crackdown on the Free
    Spirit* (Cambridge, MA: Harvard University Press, 1996).

9   A characteristic sample where this prophetic or apostolic tone is
    expressed can be found in "A Message from the Spirit of Truth
    unto the Holy Seed": "That which is set before me in the Spirit of
    Truth . . . I am moved to impart unto you, thereby to stir you up
    earnestly to press on," Nayler, *Works,* iv, p. 51.

10 It is very likely that his clarity and sophistication owe much to the

theologically insightful discourse of his allies and opponents in Cromwell's army and the dissenting churches he knew, before he ever came among Friends. Herman Melville wrote that "a whaling ship was my Yale College and my Harvard." In a similar fashion, Nayler's education was deep, but not scholastic.

11　Nayler, "What the Possession of the Living Faith Is," *Works,* iv, p. 88.

12　Nayler, Letter to George Fox and Margaret Fell (1653) in *Works,* i, p. 573.

13　Hugh Barbour (in a personal comment) has pointed out that this doctrine, widespread among Friends and others, is reminiscent of the rabbinic teaching of the evil and good tendencies, *yetzer ha-ra'* and *yetzer ha-tov.*

14　Seed can also mean "familial line" or "descendents of" as in the seed of Abraham or the seed of the serpent.

15　Nayler, "How Sin Is Strengthened, and How It Is Overcome," *Works,* iv, p. 25.

16　Cf. John Woolman: "There is a principle which is pure, placed in the human mind. . . . It is deep and inward, confined to no forms of religion nor excluded from any, where the heart stands in perfect sincerity. In whomsoever this takes root and grows, of what nation soever, they become brethren in the best sense of the expression." In *The Journal and Major Essays of John Woolman,* Phillips Moulton, ed. (New York: Oxford University Press, 1971), p. 236.

17　Nayler, "To Several Friends about Wakefield" in *Works,* i, p. 313.

18　Nayler, "A Testimony of Christ Jesus" in *Works,* iv, p. 383. Friends tended to move away from this language as the movement developed, but Nayler did not.

19　Nayler, "A Discovery of the First Wisdom from beneath and the Second Wisdom from above, or The Difference betwixt the Two Seeds The One after the Flesh, the Other after the Spirit" in *Works,* , i, p. 42.

20 Ibid, pp. 46–47.

21 John Dewey makes clear how much we are driven by the desire to make the good tarry longer, and the unpleasant or sorrowful visit less frequently. (See *Experience and Nature,* 1929.) But Koheleth (Ecclesiastes) understood it. Tenderness, or its lack, is one way of talking about what is at stake: to commit all to the "earthly life," we must harden ourselves against our mortal plight, and therefore that of others. In this way, we can neither love ourselves nor our neighbor.

22 Nayler, "A Discovery," p. 48.

23 Nayler, "Love to the Lost, and a Hand Held Forth to the Helpless to Lead out of the Dark" in *Works,* iii, p.63. This is a major theological tract worth far more study than it has received.

24 Nayler, "A Discovery," p. 52.

25 Nayler, "How Sin Is Strengthened," in *Works,* iv, p. 27.

26 Nayler, "The Lamb's War against the Man of Sin" in *Works,* iv, pp. 6–7.

27 Nayler, "How Sin Is Strengthened," p. 30.

28 Nayler, "There Is a Spirit which I Feel" in *Works,* iv, p. 382.

29 Nayler, "The Lamb's War," p. 6.

30 Nayler, "What the Possession of the Living Faith Is" in *Works,* iv, pp. 90–91.

31 Nayler, "To Friends about Holderness" in *Works,* i, p. 266.

32 Nayler, "Milk for Babes, and Meat for Strong Men" in *Works,* iv, p. 155.

33 Ibid, p. 156.

34 Nayler, "The Lamb's War," p. 2.

35 Nayler, "Milk for Babes," p. 143. George Whitehead, in *Sundry Books* (p. 644), has "this the first birth cannot do." Without raising any dispute about the correctness of the Quaker Heritage text, I still find the Whitehead version worth meditating on.

36 Erasmus taught that foolishness, the spirit-led life, and prophetic

living are somehow all facets of the same jewel, rooted inherently in our natures as spirit/body beings, and thus in the challenging idea of the Incarnation. See M. A. Screech, *Erasmus: Ecstasy and the Praise of Folly* (London: Penguin Books, 1980).

37   Nayler, "A Discovery," pp. 43–44.

DISCUSSION QUESTIONS

1. What does it mean to you to "mind the Light" or "live in the Cross"?

2. How do you "know the Spirit's voice," as different from your own? [See p. 5.]

3. The author asks "Why is it so hard to live up to the Light I think I have been given, and how shall I deal with failure of my good intentions?" [See p. 6.] What similar questions do you live with, and what is your experience of responding to them?

4. What are the differences between experiencing Christ as a "meaning" and the "true Word" or "voice of Christ"? Consider the quotation on page 11.

5. How would you describe in your own words the life of the "two seeds"? [See p. 12 and forward.] Does this perspective help you in your spiritual growth? Why or why not?

6. What is the "Lamb's War" and how do you see Friends engaged in this "war" today? [See p. 24 and forward.]

7. What are three responses to the Light that the author encourages? [See p. 26.] Why are they important?